Explaining LGBTQ+ Identity to Your Child

Biblical Guidance and Wisdom

Tim Geiger

New Growth Press
WWW.NEWGROWTHPRESS.COM

New Growth Press, Greensboro, NC 27404
newgrowthpress.com
Copyright © 2018 by Harvest USA

Unless otherwise indicated, Scripture quotations are taken from *The Holy Bible, English Standard Version*® Copyright © 2000; 2001 by Crossway Bibles, a division of Good News Publishers. Used by permission. All rights reserved.

Cover Design: Faceout Books, faceoutstudio.com
Typesetting and eBook: Lisa Parnell, lparnell.com

ISBN: 978-1-942572-31-2 (Print)
ISBN: 978-1-942572-32-9 (eBook)

Library of Congress Cataloging-in-Publication Data
Names: Geiger, Tim, 1968- author.
Title: Explaining LGBTQ+ identity to your child : biblical guidance and
  wisdom / Tim Geiger.
Description: Greensboro : New Growth Press, 2018.
Identifiers: LCCN 2018033366 (print) | LCCN 2018036013 (ebook) | ISBN
  9781942572329 (ebook) | ISBN 9781942572312 (saddle stitch)
Subjects: LCSH: Gender identity--Religious aspects--Christianity. | Sexual
  orientation--Religious aspects--Christianity. | Parenting--Religious
    aspects--Christianity. | Child rearing--Religious aspects--Christianity.
Classification: LCC BT708 (ebook) | LCC BT708 .S445 2018 (print) | DDC
  261.8/3576--dc23
LC record available at https://lccn.loc.gov/2018033366

Printed in India

27 26 25 24 23 22 21 20   4 5 6 7 8

Six year-old Ashley hopped off the school bus and gave her waiting mother a hug. As they turned to walk toward home, her mother Tammy eagerly questioned, "How was your first day in first grade?"

Ashley said she had a great time and that the teacher was really nice. "And Mommy," she said, "there were three new girls in my class."

"How exciting!" said Tammy. "Do any of them ride the bus with you?"

"One does. Her name's Lily."

"Wow! Maybe we could get together with her mom for a playdate. Do you think you would enjoy that?"

Ashley hesitated for a moment. A bit more softly, she said, "I think I would. But I'm a little mixed-up."

"Why's that, honey?" asked Tammy.

"Because she has two moms," Ashley replied. "I don't understand. Lily said her dad used to be a man, but now he's a woman. So she calls her mom, 'Mom' and her Dad, 'Mama.'" Ashley took a moment to collect her thoughts, and then asked with all of the innocence of a six-year-old: "Mommy, how does a boy become a girl?"

• • •

Ed and Steve had been friends ever since they met during the first day of freshman soccer tryouts. Each had been equally intimidated by the other players, who seemed so much faster and more coordinated. That was two years ago.

But over the last few months, Ed noticed that Steve had seemed to become progressively more withdrawn. It seemed as though something was bothering him, but he never shared with Ed what it was. He didn't text or ask to hang out as frequently as he once had. When Ed reached out to Steve, he noticed about half the time that his friend either didn't reply at all—which was strange—or said that he was busy.

One day when they were leaving soccer practice, Steve seemed particularly uneasy. Ed asked him what was up. Looking at his feet, Steve said that he didn't know if they could be friends anymore.

"What do you mean, man?" Ed asked. "What's wrong?"

Steve, still refusing to look up, told his friend, "I'm gay. I know you're a Christian, man, and you're probably not cool with this. I'm sorry."

Steve began to walk away, his head down. Ed started after him. "Hey man, wait up. Steve!" But even as he sprinted to keep up with his friend, he wasn't certain what he would say when he did catch up.

• • •

How will Tammy and Ed each respond to these moments of gospel opportunity? How should their walk with Christ inform their replies?

Cultural Changes and Challenges

One of the most significant cultural changes in generations has occurred since the beginning of this century. This change has taken place both in society at large as well as in the church, and it has strongly affected young people who have grown up during this transformative time.

As LGBTQ+[1] issues have increasingly stepped to the forefront of public discussion and debate, the evolution of LGBTQ+ identities and their gradual acceptance has produced a host of questions, disputes, and quandaries within the Christian community.

To most in the culture and to many in the church today, affirming those who self-identify as LGBTQ+ is seen as positive, loving, and an exercise of social justice. These LGBTQ+ allies focus on righting the wrongs of past generations, correcting injustices, and undoing "heteronormative" discrimination[2] against those who identify as LGBTQ+.

This message is not lost on children, who typically have a high view of social justice and "fairness." Many millennials, whether Christian or not (born 1980–1996) have a radically different understanding of sex, sexuality, and gender than their parents. Many members of Generation Z ("Gen Z," born after 1996), both Christian and non-Christian, have an even more developed sense of what social justice looks like for LGBTQ+ individuals.

Members of Gen Z are the first to have grown up in a culture permeated with mainstream media's views of LGBTQ+ identity. Members of this generation interact continuously with unedited social media, which often explicitly or implicitly promotes a radically self-centered view of sex, sexuality, and gender. As a result, their own worldviews have been shaped by the shifting views of the culture.

Addressing the Elephant in the Room

Before we discuss explaining LGBTQ+ identities to children, we should acknowledge the sad reality that fuels much of the distrust and conflict in the church surrounding this issue.

Far too often, our churches have not been places of hope and healing for people who have struggled with same-sex attraction (SSA) or gender identity. Whether intentionally or not, we have treated sexual sin as far worse than other type of sin. In doing so, we have often failed to give same-sex or gender-struggling persons the hope of the gospel ("[we] are justified by his grace as a gift, through the redemption that is in Christ Jesus, whom God put forward as a propitiation by his blood, to be received by faith," Romans 3:24–25a).

> **Talking Point:** Talk with your child about the best way for them to interact with and pray for people who affirm LGBTQ+ identities. Provide examples of loving, respectful, and courteous ways to talk with such people. Help your child to understand the importance of "gracious speech, seasoned with salt" (Colossians 4:6) for all, regardless of identity.

As a church, we have many times failed to love our struggling brothers and sisters well, by helping them bear their burdens and working to restore them gently (Galatians 6:1–2). We have not been a safe community for SSA-affected individuals to talk through their thoughts and feelings. Scripture affirms that one of the chief aims of the church is that Christians would work to build one another up not only in the knowledge of the Lord, but in the right application of that knowledge through living lives of repentance (1 Thessalonians 5:11; Hebrews 10:23–25).

Humbly admitting that the church has often reacted badly toward same-sex and gender strugglers is a positive and necessary step forward. Only as we grapple with our collective failure to love well can we move in repentance and grace toward a better future.

What will make the largest and most lasting impact in terms of helping same-sex and gender strugglers in the church is our willingness to care for them well by pointing them to their only hope and ours––the risen and reigning Lord, Jesus Christ. We do that through the costly medium of others-focused, God-oriented, real-time relationships. The issue of how to relate to those struggling with SSA and gender identity is a core concept that we'll explore throughout this book.

Addressing the *Other* Elephant in the Room

Another pressing reality is that a significant number of young people experience SSA and serious questions regarding their gender. In fact, your child has at least a one-in-ten chance of struggling with these issues him or herself.[3]

Because of how central this issue is in our culture today, it's important to approach your children with a prayerful heart as you begin this ongoing conversation. One pitfall you will want to consciously avoid is communicating shame, disgust, or rejection of those who self-identify as LGBTQ+.

Avoiding censure of the LGBTQ+ community follows Christ's example of loving the outsider and drawing them into fellowship with himself (Matthew 9:10–12). God's people are called to treat others with respect and compassion (see Colossians 4:5–6). Avoiding condemning words or attitudes toward the LGBTQ+ community will also help you avoid communicating to your child that there is something wrong with *them* if they struggle with these issues. To do otherwise may inadvertently drive an invisible wedge between you and your child, making them less likely to ask you for help with their struggles and more likely to believe they are somehow less loved by you and by God.

> **Talking Point:** Ask your child if he or she has ever wondered about his or her gender or sexual orientation. Engage them on that topic. Help him or her to talk with you and to trust that you will not reject your child because of questions or struggles.

One of the best things you can do to help the young people in your life understand LGBTQ+ identities and struggles is to model the compassionate concern of our Savior for those who are lost in sin (for example, see Hosea 11:1–9 and Matthew 23:37). Speak the truth in love to them by letting them know that any sexual behavior outside of God's good design is sin (see 1 Corinthians 6:12–20), but that God is a good and gracious God, who delights in forgiving sin and granting grace to walk in repentance (see Psalm 103:8–13). Let them know that you, too, need God's grace and forgiveness, and that is why you are committed to walking humbly with others as they endeavor to live by repentance and faith.

How Many People Self-Identify as LGBTQ+?

Studies conducted in the late 1990s and early 2000s have shown that as many as 11 percent of adolescents and young adults can struggle with significant SSA.[4] However, most of these adolescents have historically not adopted a gay or lesbian identity upon entry into adulthood. The reason? They realized, as they exited their teen years, that they were not primarily sexually attracted to others of their own gender.

More recent studies focusing on Gen Z (those born after 1996) have shown a dramatic change in self-identification, however. One study shows that only 48 percent of Gen Z respondents self-identify as "completely heterosexual," while 35 percent self-identify as "completely bisexual," and 6 percent self-identify as "completely homosexual."[5] Though this particular survey comprised a relatively small number of respondents, it reflects other recent trends. Today's adolescents

> **Talking Point:** Talk with your child about the role of sex and sexuality in his or her life. Sexuality wasn't given to us by God to relate to other people in a general sense. It is a very special aspect of our created nature, meant to be exercised in a very specific relationship: covenant marriage between one man and one woman.

have a much more fluid view of sex, sexuality, and gender than previous generations.

How about transgender (trans) young people? How many are there? Trans teens are a small minority, but the size of that group is growing. The journal *Pediatrics* published a 2016 study of 81,000 teens showed that 2.7 percent of respondents self-identified as "transgender, genderqueer, genderfluid, or unsure about [their] gender identity." Roughly twice the number of girls self-identified as gender nonconforming than did boys.[6]

Among American adults, a 2016 Gallup poll showed that 4.1 percent self-identified as LGBTQ+. That represents a 21.1 percent increase over just four years. LGBTQ+ identification remained stagnant during that period among adults over the age of forty. All of the increase in the numbers of those self-identifying as LGBTQ+ is attributed to millennials, of whom 7.3 percent now self-identify as LGBTQ+.[7]

What Does the Bible Say about Gender?

Scripture tells us that God created all of his image-bearers as either male or female (Genesis 1:27). There is nothing in the Bible that leads one to conclude that gender is distinct from birth sex, or that gender is on a continuum from male to female, or that gender evolves over the course of time. Babies born boys in Scripture are called boys from birth and grow up to be men. Babies born girls grow up to be women. Birth sex and gender, according to Scripture, are one and the same concept.

Not only did God create two genders to bear his image, but he assigned each of his image-bearers one of the two genders. In Psalm 139:13–16, we see a tender and intimate rendering of the fact that God "knitted [us] together" in our mothers' wombs,

> **Talking Point:** Help your child understand that no one can *really* change genders. People can change how they look and how they act—but on the inside, where it counts, they remain the same.

and that he wrote in his book every one of our days before one of them came to be. Gender is not something that develops as a psychological process. It is ordained by God from beyond eternity.

Our God is a marvelous and all-wise Creator who created each of us male or female because of specific ways that our gender reflects his glory to the world and heavenly realm. As boys grow to be men, with their unique and diverse talents (not all men are alike!), they reflect God's character and power in particular

> **Talking Point:** God created only two genders, and each person fully possesses one or the other. A person's gender is the same as his or her birth sex.

ways. As girls grow to be women, with their unique and diverse talents (not all women are alike, either!), they too reflect God's character and power in particular ways.

When male and female come together in marriage, there is a unique bond between the two. God tells us that husband and wife "become one flesh" (Genesis 2:24) in a particular way that (dimly) mirrors the relationship that the Son will one day share with his bride, the church (Ephesians 5:31–32).

To blur the lines between male and female, or to say that God's works in creation and providence are either wrong or insufficient, is sinful. Scripture tells us that God is right in all his works (Hosea 14:9). It also counsels us that as creatures, we lack the right to tell our Creator that he doesn't have the right to tell us how we should live (Isaiah 29:16). Simply put, God is the only one capable of designing and assigning gender to his creatures. Perhaps then, if we perceive an incongruity between birth sex and gender, we should question our own understanding of God's design.

Where Does a LGBTQ+ Identity Come From?

One of the foundational questions to examine with your child is: In light of Scripture, how do we interpret and respond to LGBTQ+ identity? What is at the root of that identity, and what is the typical process through which an individual comes to the realization that a LGBTQ+ identity is for him or her?

The two main patterns of sexual behavior at work in an LGBTQ+ identity are SSA and transgenderism. Contrary to what might seem intuitive, SSA is not primarily a function of sexual desire. And transgenderism is not primarily a function of gender. Both are products of worshipping something other than God. The Bible calls this idolatry.

Idolatry happens in each of us when certain desires become so important to us that we stop at nothing to fulfill them. We read in James 1:14–15:

> But each person is tempted when he is lured and enticed by his own desire. Then desire when it has conceived, gives birth to sin, and sin when it is fully grown brings forth death.

James tells us here that what really is at the root of all our sinful behavior, and the temptation that leads to sin, is the desire in our own hearts. *Desire—or more precisely, controlling desire—is what leads to sin of all types.*

What are some of those desires? Here is a diagram that illustrates some of the more typical ones, and the process through which they become idols.

How Desires Become Idols

Desire		Idol
Love Good self-image Affirmation Affection Security No pain or suffering Control Comfort Understanding Intimacy	Disappointment Discouragement Despair	"I must have this...I don't care what it takes"

The process usually looks something like this:

1. A person experiences a desire that is not satisfied in the way they want (or, not satisfied at all).
2. Typically, such a person repeatedly experiences that desire not being met as anticipated. As they experience repeated disappointment over their desire not being met, they begin to experience discouragement and eventually despair. They begin to believe they will never receive the anticipated outcome.
3. That person then reaches the conclusion that the unsatisfied desire is of such great importance to them that they are willing to do anything to satisfy it. By this point, the person is so tired of waiting that they are willing to do whatever is necessary to get their desires met.

None of the ten categories of desire listed on the left side of the diagram appear to be, in and of itself, evil. And, you'll note, none of these desires has any direct connection to sex or gender. In fact, all of these desires are part of who we are created to be as God's image-bearers.

> **Talking Point:** Help your child reflect on specific ways in which he or she is tempted to sin. Help him or her begin to understand the link between underlying desire and temptation in his or her own life.

However, sin has distorted and corrupted everything we are and want. Sin has tainted our own desires. It has corrupted the ways in which we want those desires to be met. It has impacted the systems that God has established in human community (families, the church, friendships, government, culture itself).

Sin has impacted the nature of these desires. The right and holy fulfillment of each of these desires is intended to, in some way, bring glory to God. However, distorted by sin, they all become profoundly turned inward. Instead of asking, "How can I love others and receive love from God?" the question becomes, "How can I get this person to demonstrate their love for me?" Instead of asking, "How can I affirm and build up this other person?" the question becomes, "Will they notice me?"

Where do sex and gender come into this discussion? Because everything about us is distorted by the power of sin, sex and gender become means to the end of getting these desires met. Quite simply put, sexual and gender-related sin provides a convincing counterfeit resolution for each of these desires. It deceives the person into thinking they've actually received what will bring them life and satisfaction.

Such patterns of behavior linked to desire don't form overnight. Many who experience SSA or gender struggles first deal with these unmet desires in childhood. When they become sexually aware in adolescence (or, when sexualized at an earlier age), sex or gender identity becomes a way to compensate for the losses they experience in relation to these desires.

Neither SSA nor transgender is initially an orientation, but it *becomes* an orientation as the

> **Talking Point:** Help your child understand how easily we can be deceived by the sinful desires of our own hearts. Talk about experiences from your own life about the deceptive nature of sin, and how easy it is to believe lies about yourself, others, and God.

individual repeatedly gives him or herself over to these desires. Through doing so, he or she builds a cause-and-effect response pattern in his or her brain.

At some point in the development of these sin patterns, the individual may come to the point at which he or she realizes that the greatest number of desires can be satisfied most easily at the least relational cost through adopting a LGBTQ+ identity. In other words, landing on a LGBTQ+ identity is a way for an individual to find maximum coherence and significance as an individual.

Another factor in the long process of adopting LGBTQ+ identity is the search for community. As individuals who struggle with SSA and gender try to find an accepting and affirming community, they often perceive that they will have a greater possibility of finding such community in the LGBTQ+ community, among others who, at least in this one area that has come to dominate their own sense of identity, are most like themselves.

How would you pray for anyone seeking counterfeit satisfaction for their desires? You'd ask that the Lord would lead them to find the *lasting* satisfaction of their desires through humble reliance upon God. You'd ask the Lord to help them exercise *self-control*, because they understand at a heart level who God is, and that he loves them and can help them turn away from the impulse to intuitively satisfy a desire through sexual or gender-related sin patterns. Learning and practicing the biblical concept of *contentment in Christ, regardless of one's circumstances* (Philippians 4:4–13) also helps one turn from the instinctual "need" to satisfy a desire in the moment, through sin.

However, breaking patterned systems of desire-and-response that have become established over the course of years takes time. And, it takes

> **Talking Point:** Help your child think through ways to pray for LGBTQ+ identified people to find real contentment not in their identities, but in God alone, and that the community of God's people—the church—would grow in grace to become a safe and welcoming place for them to seek that contentment.

help. Strugglers need patient brothers and sisters to come alongside them and encourage them to grow in their understanding of God's love, and to hold them accountable for their desires and behavior.

Explaining LGBTQ+ Identity in Age-Appropriate, God-Glorifying Ways

LGBTQ+ identity, and all of the underlying counterfeit desires that help form it, is a complex concept to understand. How do you explain it to children or teens? We must talk about LGBTQ+ in age-appropriate, God-glorifying ways, providing only the information necessary for the child to understand the basics of the issue.

A six-year-old doesn't need to know all the details of LGBTQ+ behavior. But it is appropriate to explain to a six-year-old that the gay couple living down the street makes God feel sad because they're living together like two daddies, when God's Word says that married couples should be made up of one mommy and one daddy. We need to pray for them, but we also need to respect them and be kind to them as we talk with them on the street. They are our neighbors, and we're called to love them.

A twelve-year-old in the same situation can handle more information: This is *why* a gay couple living together is wrong—because God created man and woman to reflect his image in a particular way when they become one in marriage, and it's fundamentally impossible for two men or two women to reflect that image without distorting it.

In other words, you don't need to use sexually explicit language at any age level to explain SSA—nor should you. In addition, you should be careful to paint SSA as a struggle that many people experience. Paul tells us that there is no temptation except that which is common to man (1 Corinthians 10:13).

Similarly, when talking about trans people to your child, it doesn't need to be exhaustive: just enough for your child to understand how to think about the issue from a biblical perspective. A six-year-old with a trans classmate needs to know there is an inherent goodness to gender that God created, and that there are only two genders. The gender someone is born with is his or her real, lifelong gender. People don't have the right to change something that God made just because they're not happy with it. The trans classmate is someone who has made a wrong decision (a decision likely encouraged by misguided adults in his or her life) about how to live. And we are called to love other sinners, just as Jesus loves us.

One way to show that love is to pray for that classmate, that the Lord would give them a true understanding of his or her gender and take control his or her heart. Another way to love that other person is to befriend him or her, and to affirm them in what they look like on the *inside*—not just on the outside.

> **Talking Point:** Explain to your child that being someone's friend doesn't mean that you agree with everything they do or believe. Use your relationship with Jesus as an example: Jesus loves you, even though you still struggle with sin against him.

A twelve-year-old in similar circumstances can process more information. You might want to explain the foundational concept of idolatry, and encourage your twelve-year-old to get to know his or her classmate well enough to begin to pray for and speak truth in love into some of those places of idolatry.

What does it mean to speak the truth in love in these situations? Simply put, it means two things. First, always get to know the person and his or her story before speaking into his or her situation. As we examined earlier, the development of an LGBTQ+ identity is a process—and frequently, a long and painful one for the individual. In order to earn the

> **Talking Point:** If your child knows someone who self-identifies as LGBTQ+, they must earn the right to speak into his or her life. Listen to the struggler's story. Look for ways to compassionately shine the light of truth into that person's life. Become a real friend to anyone you would speak to in this way.

right to speak ("to help the other person see [his or] her life clearly"), we must first get to know that person as a person, and humbly grow to love him or her as a fellow image-bearer.[8]

Second, we recognize that we are fellow sinners, and therefore don't have the moral high ground from which to criticize and condemn. We quite humbly speak the truth about God and his salvation, in *love*. As recipients of God's love through Jesus Christ, we are called to share what we have received with others. To quote Martin Luther, "We are all mere beggars telling other beggars where to find bread."

Speaking the truth in love also entails having compassion and empathy for the other person. We should not do this out of pity, but because that other person is a fellow image-bearer of God—an image-bearer whose own sense of self and God has been clouded by sin. As those who know the Lord and his salvation, we should prayerfully, patiently, and lovingly seek to engage others who need to know him as we do. That sort of engagement happens through authentic friendship.

Practical Ways to Practice the Love and Grace of Jesus

Here are some practical ways to help your child understand how to live out grace and compassion with LGBTQ+ identified individuals:

1. Adopt a zero-tolerance policy on bullying. Bullying has no place among God's people. We are called not to exploit the differences of others, but to love them because God himself first loved us (see Luke 10:25–37). If your child observes bullying, ask him or her to bring the information to you or to another trusted adult. Silence about bullying enables the bully to continue.

2. Talk proactively with your child about idolatry. Using the *How Desires Become Idols* diagram on page 13, help your own child to understand his or her own idols and how he or she turns to sin as a way to meet those desires illegitimately. Help your child to see that their sin has the same roots as the sin of others (James 1:13–15).

3. Help your child to pursue repentance for his or her own sin. Encourage him or her to follow the course of contentment and truth Paul speaks of in Philippians 4:4–13. Help them to understand that true repentance is only possible by God's grace (Romans 2:4), and that the pursuit of holiness must take

place within the context of community (i.e., with a friend).

4. Pray with your child for the person they know who is LGBTQ+ identified. Help your child pray that this person would know the full power of God's love, grace, and mercy, and that he or she would walk in repentance—not just of his or her LGBTQ+ identity, but of any idolatry and unbelief in his or her life (Ephesians 2:1–10).

5. Create ways for your child to interact with their LGBTQ+ friend/neighbor. If the other person is a classmate, ask that individual and his or her parents to come to your home for a play date, coffee, or dinner. Get to know this friend and his or her family. Interact with them, and simply through your generosity of friendship, reflect the love of God into their lives (see Jesus's example in Matthew 9:10–13).

6. Show respect yourself for the LGBTQ+ identified person. Your child will take cues from your conduct and pattern their words and behavior after your own (Ephesians 4:29).

7. Practice ways for your child to speak to the LGBTQ+ identified individual. Role-play simple conversations that your child might have, in which he or she talks with the other person about Jesus and the hope that he or she has in him (Colossians 4:2–6).

8. Don't tolerate coarse joking, name-calling, or other discriminatory acts in your own spheres. God's people are called to a different standard (see Ephesians 4:29 and 5:1–4).

9. Invite the LGBTQ+ identified person to join you in church and church-related activities (home group, youth group, Sunday school, Bible studies, etc.) (Romans 10:13–14).

10. Encourage your child to be committed to love the LGBTQ+ person for the long haul. What God is after is that person's heart. Often, patterns of sin that have taken hold over the course of years take years to fall apart. Even if change never happens, we are still called to love and persevere with the other person (2 Peter 3:8–9).

Endnotes

1. The "Q" in the acronym stands for "Queer," a term referring to individuals whose lifestyles do not clearly fit criteria for lesbian, gay, bisexual, or transgender identities. The plus sign at the end is meant to broadly include others who self-identify with lifestyles outside these five spectra.

2. *Heteronormativity* is the social-science term applied to cultural practices that assume that heterosexuality and a male-female gender binary system are normative. For an overview of a non-heteronormative viewpoint, see www .goodtherapy.org/blog/psychpedia/heteronormativity.

3. Gary Remafedi, et al., 1992, "Demography of Sexual Orientation in Adolescents." *Pediatrics*, 89 (4),

714–721. Given the shame-based nature of SSA, many adolescents who experience it may choose to not self-disclose such attraction. Therefore, it is the author's opinion that the actual percentage of SSA-struggling adolescents may be higher.

4. Ibid.

5. Shepherd Laughlin, "Gen Z Goes Beyond Gender Binaries in New Innovation Group Data," March 11, 2016, J. Walter Thompson Innovation Group, www.jwt intelligence.com/2016/03/gen-z-goes-beyond-gender-binaries-in-new-innovation-group-data (last accessed 02/19/2018).

6. David Roach, "Transgender Teens: New Study 'No Surprise,' Says Ethicist," Baptist Press, bpnews.net /50486/transgender-teens-new-study-no-surprise-says-ethicist (last accessed 03/07/2018).

7. Gary J. Gates, "In U.S., More Adults Identifying as LGBT," Gallup, news.gallup.com/poll/201731/lgbt-identification-rises.aspx (last accessed 03/16/2018).

8. Paul David Tripp, *Instruments in the Redeemer's Hands* (P&R Publishing, Phillipsburg, NJ, 2002), 111. Chapters 6–14 in this book do an excellent job of describing the incarnational ministry of humbly and compassionately walking alongside someone struggling with a pattern of sin.